Ghost Man on Second gives us grief and endurance, loss and joy, transmuted by the play of verse and imagination into poetry. Its thematic concerns deal with an absent father, suggested by the book's title, the troubles and determination of a young mother alone, and how these conditions have affected their child. Dilemmas, hurts, yearnings, and elusive retrievals are magically changed by the poet's sophisticated technical skill into living poems, works of art that invite reading and rereading. New forms, like the duplex, and old, like the sonnet sequence, offer us strong feeling and fresh wisdom and the remembered sense that these have always been what we expect from well-wrought poems. As the poet implies in one of her best, what is behind and above the artificial ceiling are forgotten depths of space and light. And the aim of our imaginary self wandering the world is eventually to make it home.

Mark Jarman, author of *Zeno's Eternity*
2023 Donald Justice Poetry Prize Judge

It is rare for a poet's first book to arrive fully formed and perfectly made, like Athena bursting spear in hand from the forehead of Zeus. In recent years, that rare company might include Kaveh Akbar, Natalie Diaz, Robin Coste Lewis, and Ocean Vuong, and now Erica Reid joins them. And so like Athena, Reid's speaker must deal with an absent mother (making her long for "any mother's touch, even if she's a myth") and a father who has at least passed on a superpower before exiting her life altogether. That superpower is the concept of the "Ghost Man on Second"—and you'll just have to read this stunning collection (half in free verse, half in form, and wholly in love with language) to find out more.

Julie Kane, author of *Mothers of Ireland*

"Sometimes a girl must shatter," Erica Reid writes, and there is definitely a shattering in these sharp, incisive, and tender poems. Formally ambitious and emotionally expansive, this book will take its readers on a journey—like that of this collection's eponymous ghost man—a journey toward and away from home.

Matthew Olzmann, author of *Constellation Route*

The speaker of the poems that compose Erica Reid's *Ghost Man on Second* is well-acquainted with chaos and its antidote—"the diamond- / shaped cycle" of form, the capacity to tell the tale, to name, and poetry's cradling music. The array of forms—from the golden shovel to the ghazal, the cat's cradle sonnet to the sonnet crown that is situated in the belly of the book—is illuminative. One feels form's necessity, the pressure of truth upon it. Each formal experiment provides a nest for the ghost, the angel, and the neglected child that haunt this book. Now and then, a rough upbringing and its consequent emptiness can incite a rare capacity for seeing and chronicling what is. "The trees' white pulp is so thick on the trail / that my eyes first choose to believe / a rabbit's warren has been ripped apart— / all that sacred belly fur scattered," Reid writes, forever transforming the way I will see a cottonwood, a rabbit warren, and a poem. This is a book to reread and cherish.

Diane Seuss, author of *frank: sonnets* and *Modern Poetry*

Ghost Man on Second

GHOST MAN ON SECOND

Erica Reid

AUTUMN
HOUSE PRESS

pittsburgh

ISBN: 978-1-637680-81-0

Cover Art: Tandem X Visuals. "White bird on a brown tree branch."
Book Design: Chiquita Babb
Author Photo: Ben Bradley

Library of Congress Cataloging-in-Publication Data

Names: Reid, Erica (Arts marketer), author.
Title: Ghost man on second / Erica Reid.
Identifiers: LCCN 2023046619 (print) | LCCN 2023046620 (ebook) | ISBN
    9781637680810 (paperback) | ISBN 9781637680865 (epub)
Subjects: BISAC: POETRY / Women Authors | POETRY / Subjects & Themes /
    Death, Grief, Loss | LCGFT: Poetry.
Classification: LCC PS3618.E5346 G45 2024 (print) | LCC PS3618.E5346
    (ebook) | DDC 811/.6--dc23/eng/20231030
LC record available at https://lccn.loc.gov/2023046619
LC ebook record available at https://lccn.loc.gov/2023046620
Printed in the United States on acid-free paper that meets the international standards of
permanent books intended for purchase by libraries.

pennsylvania
COUNCIL ON THE ARTS

GREATER PITTSBURGH
ARTS COUNCIL

Arts loud and clear

Autumn House Press is a nonprofit corporation
whose mission is the publication and promotion
of poetry and other fine literature. The press
gratefully acknowledges support from individual
donors, public and private foundations, and
government agencies. This book was supported,
in part, by the Greater Pittsburgh Arts Council and the
Pennsylvania Council on the Arts, a state agency funded by the
Commonwealth of Pennsylvania, and the National Endowment
for the Arts. To find out more about how National Endowment
for the Arts grants impact individuals and communities, visit
www.arts.gov.

The Donald Justice Poetry Prize:
The Donald Justice Poetry Prize is part of the Spencer Poetry Awards, which Kean W. Spencer
created in 2005 in honor of his mother, Iris N. Spencer. The prize recognizes the distinguished
American poet, teacher, and Pulitzer Prizewinner, Donald Justice, one of the finest poets of the
late twentieth century.

CONTENTS

Home

Ghost Man on Second

Ghost Man on Second

My dad had too few kids to field wiffle ball, so
he introduced me to the Ghost Man. Suppose
I found myself stuck at second base
when it came my turn to bat: The Ghost Man
could take my place, continuing my parade
around the bases.
                         Of all the ghosts
my parents left to me, this Ghost Man
serves me best—see the hurled ball
pass right through him, watch him score
a shred of glory in my name. Long after dusk
has eaten the Midwestern backyard
barely large enough to hold this game,
years after the players have gathered
the Frisbee & pie-plate bases & have gone
their separate ways, the Ghost Man runs—
is still running—through the diamond-
shaped cycle that I taught him: toward & away
from home, toward & away from home.

FIRST

Disorder

A recent season of dreams has made it clear
that I prefer a hellscape where I understand the rules
to a paradise where I do not.

How can it be a paradise
if even here I cannot make my mother smile? No—
I am forced to ring the winged bellhop & say: *Sorry
to trouble you but this must be a web of someone else's
desires.* I hold a single hope. It takes very little to see
that this heaven is not for me.

In a better dream, a meteor
whacks the earth like a chocolate orange.
While my eighth-grade classmates quake & scramble
I stand at the head of the school bus, shouting
through the bullhorn I seem to carry in dreams:

This is what finally frightens you? No—
chaos & I go way back. I will chart our path, teach you
what I have lived. Now lace up the Magma Boots
I asked you to bring, line up according to height. Follow me

into hostile terrain. If the terror feels overwhelming,
step one is to give it a name.

Five-Story House

Ground

Everything begins, somehow. I wish I could remember
the moment before I began to hurt this way. There was
a time when my body held no secrets. How did my blood
move through me in those days? My guess is easily,
without a second thought.

Second

I never had a bedroom at my father's house. For a time,
before he remarried, he laid a mattress on the floor
& it was mine. When he built his own house, it had a room
for my brother, another for my sister, another for my
stepmom's treadmill.

Third

Yesterday I had a waking dream in which my inner child
untethered herself from me like an astronaut abandoning
her space walk, floating adrift. If she feels that way now,
I felt that way back then. I can remember if I close my eyes.
I try not to close my eyes.

Fourth

I tell my husband I want my own bedroom & he laughs,
not unkindly. He knows I ache for a space no one can take
from me. I would accept my own mattress on the floor.
We compromise: I choose new pillows & on Mondays
I sleep alone on the couch.

Rooftop

I believed I'd see clearly from here. Have I not climbed
high enough yet, am I not far from being a child? Inside,
my blood gets stuck in old places. I have never felt new.
I keep angling for a glimpse of my whole self, but
all the taller houses block the view.

Each Night I Send My Courage Out

I could sleep if it weren't for this body. At 2 I am
a rod of platinum in a plastic sack of dry leaves.

    When do we outgrow our cradles? Too early we become
    responsible for our sleep, as though it were easy

        to set down the ratchets & grapples of the body, gag
        white arctic winds of the mind. It is the child in me

    awake tonight. I see her, I never go to her, I do not
    stand by her bed to lure her fears into bottles. No

mother shows up in me. Each night I send my courage out
to hunt for one, knowing the search will turn up only

    more cold. I say, *You must grow tough, sweet girl.* Soon
    enough you will kick & twist in the empty arms of these hours

        while you blame your restless legs, your back, any pain
        that feels easy to claim. The way your knees ache after rain.

Sestina Obbligato

The orchestra ambushes me with Mahler's Fifth.
I never played; I have no innate sense of music
so it's a shock to feel the brass ransack my body.
Stop I rasp when the trumpets make my edges blur
& a solo horn tugs my soul through my throat.
Stop. You need permission to touch me this way.

⌒

I'm not lost, I just know this isn't the way.
I have my landmarks—the clock tower on Fifth,
the bronze fountain where you ogled my throat,
a bank that was a Friendly's. To me, places are music,
shifting & resolving. Maps make my eyes blur,
but I can get you where you need to go. Ask anybody.

⌒

Every day is a negotiation with my body—
to love or not to love, to weigh or not to weigh?
I long to be a head in a jar or a quick blur
of binary in a B-cupped android. Oh yes, the fifth-
generation model with no lag, lithe legs, pop music
streaming from a discrete vent hidden in the throat.

⌒

My mother left the dentist with bruises on her throat
& collarbone, yellow-green. He'd pushed her body
for leverage as, against a background of tinny Muzak,
he yanked at her wisdom teeth. Or that's the way
she explained it to me—I only caught every fifth
word, anesthesia making her story blur.

Dear F—, did my letter reach you, did rain blur
my return address? Did my note slip down the throat
of the sewer, is it sitting in a distant pool of filth,
unopened? Short of that, I can't imagine somebody
reading what I wrote & not responding. I can wait.
Maybe you're tied up, maybe you're too sick.

Erato, Urania? Which of the brave muses
will claim my janky poems, the ones that blur
comedy & bruise, elegy & sway?
Calliope, send your sister to grip me by the throat
until truth steams from every vent in my body.
I'll take any mother's touch, even if she's a myth.

In music, the obbligato must be played precisely the way
it was written. In the body—in the throat—the same is true.
We recite our page (no blur, no shift) for the fourth time. For the fifth.

Invitation

Father's Day again. Dads, I'm not impressed.
I've had 3—more if you count the men
who saw me reaching, held me to their chests,

vamoosed before we passed the sack race test.
Don't cry for me—I'm 38—but when
somebody ditches me I'm 9 again,

standing at my kitchen window, dressed
for Easter Sunday in December, since
last April you said you liked this outfit best.

Dads, don't let me keep you from your gin,
the round of golf you're trying to fit in,
your gifts—a tie, a hammer, who'd have guessed—

but once your cake's been cut, might I suggest
you stop a moment, truly drink it in,
reflect upon your list of party guests.

Was there one invitation unaddressed?
A card for the other daughter, who ran west—
the only heart you never welcomed in?

Duplex for the Noonday Demon

Shake a man, when you can, by his ribs.
Time is a cracked egg on a slick skillet.

    Tomorrow's a slick egg on a cracked skillet.
    I have been socking away days on the sly.

I have been pocketing days on the sly,
picking noon's lock with a hairpin.

    Restless, I pick your locks with hairpins.
    We are out of secrets, so we pester birds.

We pester birds to give up their secrets.
Why do we name angels but not vultures?

    We name our angels but never our vultures
    though both circle emptiness from above.

Love, do you sense an emptiness circling us?
Shake a man, when you can, by his ribs.

Pelt

This molding coat I'm wearing—this *mood*—
this chewed-up mink, this blessed heavy mess
with its wet kinks, with its whiffy kiss of sweat,

this mood, all its gnarls, its curls, its age-old
burrs, this wretched sable, this fetching ruin,
thick hulk funking its bulk in my rough shape—

ratty mood! Menace in its drape, its feeble sag,
my drowsy cape. Sleeves uneven, buttons like
loose teeth. And me with nothing underneath.

Why Is My Angel So Small?

Nice girl, one hell of a dancer, but only as tall
as a deck of cards. Hard for her to help me much—
to block the blows, to shield me from what is being
thrown. She can hold a secret & that's about all.

In the fall, when my 4-inch angel arrived,
I fashioned a frock from my quilt discards, a basin
out of a bottle cap, a bed from an anchovy tin. Why
am I the one doing all of the tucking in?

My pocket protector loves cashews, apple slices,
bites of my cake. I give her whatever keeps her
bright & smiling. It feels cruel, but I wonder
if she will grow—or if I am meant to get smaller.

To tell you the truth, I had hoped to be held.
I wished to be swaddled & not to be needed,
to have the chance to be the child this time around.
Yet here I am again, in a too-familiar land,

where the one meant to take care of me is eating from my hand.

Nocturne after Kelly Weber

There are things I can only say at night. I hang
a dinner plate for a moon. Soon morning will crack
my illusion with her broken fingers. I call this ritual.
Kelly says *we don't owe anyone anything.* Still
I was swaddled into a world of owing. There is a tooth
in the word *indentured,* contracts ripped ragged.
When I ripped my mother open, our contracts
matched. That was that. My life borrowed against
before I knew how to bat my eyes. This porcelain moon
can't pull a tide. Nothing shifts inside me. Waves lap
a concrete shore. If anything green sprouts through the cracks,
salt water takes it back. To grow would be to mother.
My body snaps vines like fingers. Hemlock & cement.
Once I met a church. His doors were wide open.
He said *you don't owe anyone anything.* Doors wide like
traps. I need to understand the economy. The rate of exchange.
My worth is asleep under a blanket strewn with teeth.
If I move, I'll break a smile across this floor. Hunger
is different from emptiness. I'd need to know what I want
to be hungry. There are things I can only want at night. And
here comes a new day's light, crooked at each knuckle.

Links

Years, years! This is what it has come to:
I mailed a letter & the answer was bored silence.
My father etc. would rather not read &
I honested myself out of his family photo.
My grandfather died & nobody told me.
I discover so much by accident.

My grandfather died & nobody told me.
What is a grandfather anyway?
Only a father's father, right? How many do I need?
How many can I bore to death? Bye, Walter—
I didn't get to tell you what you never asked
& your great-grandkids would not have played football.

How many do I need? This suitcase is small
so I choose my best books & the clock on the wall.
I'm not running—no one is looking for me—
I am preparing for fire. If you don't start one I will.
Might as well do something worth being blamed for.
I sold my father's watch. He never owned a watch.

If you don't start a daisy chain, I will.
Don't try to keep me from ruthlessly flowering.
This isn't his field. He never owned a field.
You will not find your copper coins here, grandfather.
You did not drop your silver watch here, father.
The only loose change in this field is me, face like a dime.

Daguerreo

Am I the I in my poems? Here is what I know: *I*
cannot look my mother in the eye anymore, I *am*
scared skinless. It's more than her iodine smile, *not*
only her whip hands, dagger hips, not even *the*
bone-deep soul-note her throat blows, no. *I*
am terrified of the tiny tintype she tucks *in*
her sock drawer. It keeps me small. Inside *my*
writing, we touch noses. I grow right up in *poems.*

Father as Ghost or Sheep or Nothing

Though I have not heard from you in 6 years, mom *in*
-sists that someday, when a relative passes to me *the*
news of your illness—word that you have some *form*
of cancer, something even the doctors are afraid *of*
—that we will mend fences. She believes there is *a*
daughter muscle, deep in me, stronger than the *black*
spots where wind whistles through my love. The *ewe*
can only see the lamb in the lamb. I'm not so sure—*my*
softness is a memory. How could you be more of a *ghost*
than you were yesterday? Father, I suppose we *will*
find out together. And if something dark does *straggle*
into your system, if a knotted disease starts moving *through*
your heart, we will have that in common. Wait. I bet *your*
mind skips over me in your last dreams, as in all your *dreams*.

Wake-up Call

Nine years after I leave the nest
I find myself an awkward guest
in mother's new apartment—when
I land in my hometown, she lends
                her second bedroom.

This spare room has facilities
which mom keeps stocked with niceties:
musky soaps carved into blossoms,
tiny toothpastes, little flosses,
                mint-ginger shampoo,

each one sealed with a hotel crest.
These travel-gathered gifts suggest
my mother's style of invitation:
Feel welcome on this brief vacation
                but check out by noon.

The Earth Has Hiked Her Skirt

and stepped around me into spring.
Ducks changed guard, all widgeons now.
Nothing goes at my pace. Nothing waits.

In January I knew every birdcall on this trail.
There were only two birdcalls to know.
One of them was mine, & more of a cry.

Who fired the pistol? Who said we were ready
for song? My loneliness is a frog still sleeping
but white pelicans are buzzing the tower

& I'm tripping over everything's beginning.
Persephone must be home again, pj'd in her
childhood bed below a pushpinned poster

of Billie Joe Armstrong.   Good for her.
Good for the daughters with rooms waiting.
For some of us, winter is as close as we get

to the romance of a secret second life.
Our inch-thick rivers thaw & move away.
Will no one protest this coming of joy?

Too late, a brisk chill limps through the air.
I swear it strokes my hair as it goes.

Shucking

On New Year's Eve, mom & I booked a place
downtown. She wore a mollusk-colored dress, open
at the back, & heels she knew she could move
in. Our dinner plans were too early—we had to stall
so we could mark the hour with champagne fizz.
We sucked down oysters shipped from a distant sea.

In Ohio, you're a full day's drive from the nearest sea.
Growing up, the Great Lakes were an exotic place—
three hours, as far as my family could drive without fist-
fights in the back seat, mom cranking the window open
& chucking out the Hot Wheels car my brothers & I all
wanted. *Nothing left to fight over.* Her signature move.

Lately I've been watching my life like it's a movie
that a neighbor is playing with the curtains wide; I see
blue light & the movements of fight scenes, that's all.
None of this is happening to me, I have no place
in this film. My neighbor has left the drapes open
again—another poor actress at the business end of a fist.

In my house, it was the women who put their fists
into drywall, who slammed doors & moved
through hallways like wild horses. At 13, I had only to open
my glossy mouth to set us off. Even now I never see
it coming—the toss of the head, the breakneck pace.
I used to think she was the only mad stallion in the stall.

＿＿＿＿

I will not be a mother. Certain friends tell me to stall,
too soon to decide. They cannot see that I have a fist
for a womb. I know I am missing a safe, warm place
inside. Where do I fit, a woman who does not simply move
against the current, but drifts out to her own empty sea?
Pull me back from the lonely gush, from the wide open.

＿＿＿＿

There were years when our relationship hinged open.
In these years, I took our fury & swallowed it all.
(Even in Ohio, oysters taste like the wide, blank sea.)
I was young when I understood that words can be fists
& I could either learn to dodge, weave, & move,
or else I could disappear, send a glossy decoy in my place.

＿＿＿＿

Perhaps my place in this world is trying to move
toward me—if I stall, stand stock still, pray to be seen,
a door will open like a fist, or an apology.

SECOND

Emily

It's you & me against the world, she'd say
as I was growing up, & even when
we were adults together, almost sisters
instead of mom & daughter. She & I—
well. Now it's been 4 years since we have spoken,
since that March night I tested *you & me*
and found a cold world whistling between us.
Is there a story here, or am I treading
the same ground as most mothers, many daughters?
So close, until we cross each other's boundaries.
So quick with cudgel words, so slow with *sorry*.
So often she struck last. This time, my turn—
       that night, I wheeled my suitcase out her door.
       We'd broken what we'd only bruised before.

We'd broken what we'd only bruised before
in petty skirmishes. Take driving lessons,
when mom would cover up my rearview mirror,
demand I name the color, make, & model
of vehicles behind me. If I couldn't,
she'd flop into a dark exasperation.
Too many such "mistakes"—too slow a turn,
too nervous of a merge onto the freeway—
she'd tell me to pull over, drive us home
herself, a little faster than was called for.
Eventually I stopped requesting lessons,
bummed rides from friends & took the bus to school.
        To make sure both his girls came out alive,
        my stepdad wound up teaching me to drive.

My stepdad wound up teaching me to drive,
but there was plenty only mom could do.
Age 12: The bathroom of a Burger King
found me a wailing mess, my knickers stained
not red, as I'd been warned about, but brown.
I hate the word *hysterics*, but it fits.
I fumbled tissue. How to tell my mom
a test had just begun, & I was failing?
I didn't say a word, of course. She knew
when I slumped to our lunch booth looking ashen.
She gave my younger brothers some excuse
(by instinct this felt critical). Then she—
            now armed with napkins, truth, & Tampax Pearl—
gave me her crash course on this dark new world.

My mom gave me her crash course on the world
but could not seem to teach me how to steer
around her shifting moods. Mercurial—
I never knew which mother I would get,
which daughter I should be. My stepdad patched
the wall after she swung my bedroom door
so hard the knob punched through, during some fight
about—well who knows what. I'm sure I said
some jackass teenage thing. This, the same mother
who entered every contest in the paper
to try to win us tickets to see *Phantom*.
Nobody loved me harder. I am trying
        not to reduce our past to a cartoon
        the way we sometimes end our myths too soon.

We tend to end Demeter's tale too soon.
This mother blistered through the halls of hell
till Hades struck a deal, returned her daughter.
And afterward? Do we believe Demeter
went back to raising wheat like nothing happened
& lit her lonely candle every winter?
A love like that cannot sit on a spice rack
between the turmeric & coriander.
A love like that's an ever-burning coal,
a red & ready ember. No, her daughter
must spend her springs in penance for her freedom,
embroidering sweet purple buds of *thank you*.

      What debt does Persephone owe Demeter, or
      is mine the only mother keeping score?

Of course, now I'm the one who's keeping score.
My mind goes to my wisdom teeth: in college
all 4 of them impacted, 2 abscessed.
The surgeon said that as extractions go
mine was a breeze; I'd done the work already
by bearing mounting pain until my teeth
had freed themselves. I convalesced at home,
expecting comfort, which mom gave at first—
at least until I failed to eat the ice cream
she'd bought especially for me. Raspberry.
She railed at me, at my ingratitude.
I changed my own red gauze, drove to my dorm.

       My roommate swiped the pain pills I stopped taking.
       It's hard to feel at home unless I'm aching.

It's hard to feel at home unless I'm aching.
I noticed this the first years of my marriage—
those years were peaceful, which I could not stomach.
To trigger fervor I thought we were lacking,
I gnawed familiar red apples of discord
—not gold, as epics warn about, but red.
To me, deep love was always laced with anger,
but he would not fight back. He let me hurt him
& would not join me there. I had to choose
to be his ally or to be his bully.
I stepped off of my mother's scorched-earth path
& followed him. He knew another way.

      I'd found a guide to lead where I was blind—
      but as I healed, did I leave her behind?

In Colorado, mom left me behind.
I'd flown out for a week—a girlfriend's wedding—
& mom had come along for fun, to help me
navigate the bright world of the bridesmaid.
The wedding was a joy, I read a poem—
but afterward, as ever, I tripped up,
dismissed her with an eye roll. Mom took off
in our shared rental car & left me stranded.
She would not speak when we met at the airport.
I tried to show her photos from the party,
she would not speak. Not through the awkward flight,
not when we wrestled luggage, drove back home.
       When finally she spoke, I plugged my ears.
       We let that silence drag on for a year.

We let these silences drag on for years,
which might as well be lifetimes for the grief
they wrench across their spans. I do not need
her heat, her anger—but I miss my mother.
For Christmas once she bought me platform shoes,
coal-black, with cruel red flames along each side.
Ugly, right? How I loved them. Nobody
could hurt me in those shoes, they were my proof
that someone saw the truth of me. She did,
she does. It's how she knows the perfect place
to land her arrow. (She taught me this aim.)
Both cut, we wait to see which one will give—
       a game as cold as fire, as old as water.
       Unstoppable mother. Immovable daughter.

Unstoppable mother, immovable daughter:
opposing forces. When Persephone
discovers she can thrive in sun *and* shadow,
where does that leave Demeter? If her daughter
starts spending time away from field & furrow
& rolls her eyes when mom asks where she's been—
if Persephone strides in with pomegranate-
red juice around the corners of her lips—
well, what was all this for? This sacrifice
Demeter made to give this girl a life
that's better than her own, one full of choices
Demeter never had a chance to make?

      Persephone, sun daughter, you've been warned:
      Hell hath no heartache like a mother scorned.

Hell hath no courage like a mother. Born
when mom was just 16, I was the challenge
she'd test her strength against. Her father said
no prom, no football games, she is your life—
but no one had to tell my mother that.
I grew in the red shadow of that truth,
her sacrifice, & knew that I would be
the one who went to prom & football games—
or, as it would turn out, art summer camps
& poorly cast productions of *The Wiz*.
She never asked me to dilute my dreams
or made me feel like I'd left her behind.
        Mom chaperoned my field trips & was able
        to pay for school supplies by waiting tables.

Mom paid for school supplies by waiting tables
at Friendly's, where she'd later meet my stepdad—
that swarthy drywall patcher/driving teacher.
He'd tucked away some photos from the '80s:
mom, stunning in her red-and-white striped work shirt,
so charismatic, which fattens up the tips
& helps to catch the eye of charming line cooks.
Is there a story here, or am I stalling?
I know we can't go back, but what I'd give
to live those days again, just scraping by,
subsisting on the fries & chocolate Fribbles
those two snuck home from work. They were still kids.
      It's easy to forget how young they were,
      & how much growing up I asked of her.

And how much growing up I ask of her
today. A few months back I wrote a letter
saying *sorry*, saying *I should have listened more—*
instead, I rolled my suitcase out your door.
But how, I also ask, can we move forward
without red anger smoldering between us?
I know that you deserved better from me,
the very person meant to love you most
in all the world. The thing I did not write
is that I deserved better from her too.
Still do. Always her daughter, part of me
keeps reaching through the hurt to find her hand.
       She read the letter but she did not answer.
       My hope has jackknifed in me, harsh as cancer.

Your fear had jackknifed in you, harsh as cancer,
when you found you were pregnant at 15.
Your father let you stay, your mother swooned—
your boyfriend went to prom & football games.
At first you called me Emily, a name
I think of as half mine, the way I think
of you most days. (You later changed your mind,
& I can't help but wonder: Would the girl
named Emily have been a better daughter?
No sense in asking. We are who we are.)
You clenched your jaw, you tucked your fear away,
you marched us into life & did not falter.

   Emily, you told your unborn girl,
   from now on: you & me against the world.

THIRD

Colorado Cottonwoods

The trees' white pulp is so thick on the trail
that my eyes first choose to believe
a rabbit's warren has been ripped apart—
all that sacred belly fur scattered.

I am not from here. Different seeds
dust the Ohio River Valley, borne
on wetter winds. Different predators stalk
more or less the same rabbits.

On this last day of June, the river is new
in the usual way. Peonies teem
on the manhandled sides of fences.
Milkweed punches up purple flails.

To the east, a postage stamp of rainbow
tells me I have grabbed a minute
of God's attention. I offer a few words
for all the rabbits who can't go home.

Of course, there had been no rabbits.
You only saw cottonwoods, I say aloud.
Once more I have carried, warm
in my fur-lined pocket, the wrong grief—

I have scoured for my own losses
in another's mess. Still facing Ohio,
I watch for the sky to shift. If anything
changes, it waits until I have moved on.

portent

three white pelicans land at watson lake

    clotho
         lachesis

                   atropos

three sisters settle   preen   stately on the jetty

    a dark shiver portions out the lake

             only   a crow crossing the 10 o'clock sun

three fates take to the lake to fish

    sniper gulls who had lived as klepto-kings shift business to shallows

three unhurried glides   chorus of dunking buckets

    the lake has never looked so like a mirror   or a hole in a myth

       trio of white lotus blossoms on a chilly lake

           we did not come to the water for answers

           do not tell us what you know

The National Register of Champion Trees

1: Crown

If you braze yourself a crown using the copper of your thoughts,
your sterling beliefs, the hot smelt of your deeds & your best self,
if these alone are your glorious alloy, how purely will your crown
shine? The earth is a kingdom. It remembers its monarchs.

2: Trunk

You are the only thing binding some people
to this world. Yes: Some days you barely feel
tied to it yourself. You do not wish to shake
one more day by the roots of its hair. But
yours is the lucky girth, the earthy bulk
someone clutches with her last strength.
Hold on for those who hold onto you.

3: Height

You believe we measure
your height by the straight
teeth of your spine, by how
close to Jupiter are your
molars. No: How do you
work that slender height,
how far will you double over
and will you look a child
in the eye, will you kneel,

will you crawl on your belly,
will you roll if you must,
can you do it all with such
regular grace you become
a waterfall, that you know
no other happiness but in
bowing?

When I Say I Am Not a Morning Person

what I mean is that I cannot work until dawn calms.
One needs a good deal of rhythm to loop a lasso
around a poem—before 9 I am all elbows
& ankles. Still I adore these clean hours, the way
frost glisters just as it glistered for my grandmother,
for her grandmother. Yawning this morning I am the horses
in this pasture: awake, but nowhere near saddle-ready. Yes,
my neighbor's pushy rooster declares the day begun—
but then, he screams only that we all wake up. I have yet
to hear him cockle what else to do. From the east
the sun stretches the taffy of my shadow, my fingers
tapering like Shockheaded Peter's. It is a gift to watch
my breath prove itself, so visibly there, Alka-Seltzer
on the air. Low on snowmelt, the river is shivering—
dice waiting to be thrown. This, the morning work I can do:
amble, admire, silently will the birds to tell me their names.
(*Chick-a-dee*, one lies.) I could wake at 6, at 5,
but all I would find is more leisure, more lazy questions
to put to the wheat that greets the first light. If you love me
do not ask me to push the plow before sunrise—
rather, allow me an hour to gather eggs. I will turn up
with a warm dozen, we can crack them like hymnals.

Deciduous

Last night I learned that human baby teeth
are also called *deciduous*, like trees
that lose their leaves. *That which falls*
or *that which sheds*. In Latin, the word
was also used to describe shooting stars
& testicles. Words have roots. Teeth do too.

⌒

Can you see how hard I'm trying not to
smash plates? My loneliness is rattling my teeth,
I'm struggling to quash it down. Starve
a fever. Does the wind ever blow the trees
so gently it hurts? Do they use a safe word?
When I pick at my itches, the pleasure feels false.

⌒

Mom, I admit I finally see it. My hair falls
into limp curls like yours when it's too
humid outside. As a child my eyes were
green, now they're more hazel. Our eyeteeth
match, though yours are straight as trees.
Yes, we look alike, down to our scars.

⌒

New telescopes keep uncovering distant stars
but I'm just trying to make it through all
the Mondays, the Thursdays. I give myself treats

for completing simple tasks—yesterday, two
Hershey's Kisses for folding towels & flossing teeth.
One for getting out of bed. One for stepping forward.

ᴖ

Rilke asked God not to say another word.
What if He had stopped after Earth & stars . . .
oh, & water—maybe lizards, birds, His umpteenth
insect? Before people, I'm saying. Before The Fall,
& The War, & The Wall, & The War Part Two.
What if He'd stopped before me, at least? But after trees.

ᴖ

Papaw would be so proud if I learned my local trees
but I can't keep them straight. I do collect tree words—
Cycad. Cambium. Hornbeam. Acacia. Heartwo-
-od. Papaw looks disappointed on his perch in the stars
as sumacs bud in spring & ginkgoes blush in fall.
Trees have roots, I shout up. *So do words.* So do teeth.

ᴖ

Beneath January stars, I can name an evergreen or two.
After all, not every tree agrees to drop its teeth.
Deciduous is the word for who lets go, as well as who falls.

Nivôse

after Jane Hirshfield

This new snow, struck by morning light,
does not confess the same color twice—

here egg cream, egg lace, fault spidering egg,
here bleached shell, here glint of promise, last dregs of deep winter,
here bone china, kingfisher's belt, second wedding pearl,
    antimacassar.

It is not what snow covers, but what it illuminates:
rumpled sheets of the front range, mule deer's route,
crown shyness, stocks of fire logs.
Fondant yielding over the cake of the world.   ·

O unfathomable fabric, sugar dusting, radical fern,
O jewelry of fox season, your mirror offers still more mirrors—

we see a dazzle of cold futures,
we see airless depths of the sky,
we see water hushing under,
we see the paths we might yet take
    made new for us, as though it were possible
    to encounter a world unspoiled by our stepping,
    as though we had been forgiven overnight.

Preface

Someone has fixed bells to the cottonwood trees.
January air moves through them like icy wire.

Someone has laid lanterns along the exposed riverbed,
their light a golden water, a suggestion of fish.

Someone has placed holly berries in each deer track,
a rosary approaching the river, bowing, & looping back.

      Someone has recently dusted the kingfisher.
      Someone has passed this way before me.

She has painted the wind with cloves.
She has been brewing pine needle tea with honey.

Was I meant to bring a gift? I riffle my pockets.
I used to carry peanuts for the crows. Instead

I drape a garland of rabbit prints across the shadows
between trees. I do not know her. I guess at her language.

Owl

He was a Great Horned Owl, one of a mated pair
that tended to crisscross my neighborhood
keening for one another. I had not heard his song

for weeks, maybe months, & autumn wildfires
were gnashing through the canyon, close enough to dust
my deck with ash. But oh—here he is now, my owl,

a pale string of patio bulbs lighting him from below
as he stretches his neck & blows his low jug-
whistle call, mostly for her, a little for me.

Haunting, how casually I summoned this owl—
as though the necklace of stars that he followed
had been restrung, guiding him into my ripening night.

Hermitage

*13 haiku using **words** provided to me as possible opposites for "hive"*

i.

honeysuckle gag
the last **echo**
of everything

ii.

vagabond cumulus, golden grays

iii.

crackling magpies ask
themselves
blue questions
alone is my season word

iv.

downpours or vows
dissonance

v.

all grasses sway
I hear them on my tongue
nectarless

vi.

library door ajar
    hum of industry

vii.

swarm envy
    to be swept up
    & wake naked

viii.

mantis maintains her blades
ronin of the plains

ix.

smoke from the **anti-hive**
wind-up bees   mock pollen

x.

peace riven as suddenly
    nobody rings
    a brass bell

xi.

     passive **asphalt**
        prints interred in tar
        yesterday, deer

xii.

        one distant violin
        follows the trail toward me
    opens my **silo** door

xiii.

    rich cream of my mind's voice
                cloister

                           pearl

Spinnaker

November clouds press, cast the lake
into a buffalo nickel, & I want to spend it—

tip it on its side, slip it through the slot
that opens in the neck of the world,

watch the grainy video the coin buys me.
Surprise me, eye in the sky: mergansers

scattered like poppy seeds, academy jet
trailing a wide white bridal train of sound

in its wake. The slug of a slate lake-nickel
only goes so far—may it run out on me

before I'm ready, bald lights snapping up
to catch me with my mouth trout-lipped.

Click, thunk. Reset mountain lake, ducks,
virgin jet. Remake clouds out of all I forget.

The Pivot of the River Duck

The mallard, when she's in the mood
to waste less effort hunting food
will turn her foot, & so deliver
her gravity against the river

and, ducking here with beak upstream,
await the flood of bugs & bream.
Food comes to her. I ought to learn
this steady & sure-footed turn—

her shift suggesting that there may
be profit in the harder way,
& as much promise as deterrent
in pushing back against the current.

North Shields Ponds

On a frigid morning I skirt the twin ponds, binoculars
in hand—but I never lift them. It is too cold
even for sparrows, it seems. No ducks on the water.

This is how I walk through the world: willing to see
whatever is not too hard to find. Whichever bird
scares itself up, opens its kimono on its own.

The ducks are nearby, of course, sleeping
in the reeds. A sun like weak tea is beginning
to discourage the ice tinfoiling the ponds,

but I won't wait. If you were still here, you would name
the bottlebrush bush I keep walking past—your eyes
on where we are going, on the dim light unfolding.

HOME

Ghazal Flying Solo

She believed I could not stay upright on my own—
such a jolt to find out I'm all right on my own.

No matter how good my book was, he said
I could not spend our honeymoon night on my own.

My niece just turned 2. I adore her, but can't
handle all of her *star light, star bright* on my own.

Medallions & Sky Club, priority boarding,
small perks for my ten thousandth flight on my own.

Will you cover for me? My alibi's a mess,
I can't keep my white lies airtight on my own.

The bookstore rents small rooms for reading alone.
On Fridays, I drain chai & write on my own.

He fears I don't need him, but when he's away
I'm too jumpy to turn out the light on my own.

Sometimes I go stag, no one cares. Other times
people stare like I'm flying a kite on my own.

No mascara, no bra, & no part of me shaved:
I shake loose when I find myself quite on my own.

My Womb as a Room on Airbnb

Romantic getaway or girls' night out?
This fresh new listing's tidy, bright, & clean;
a recent top-to-bottom renovation
which still retains the charm of '83.
You'll love the prime location: easy walk
to dining, shopping, trails along the river.
Enjoy your private entrance, access codes
arrive by text. Yes, DoorDash does deliver.
This cozy hidden gem will feel like home,
although decor is sparse—a modern look.
A room this stunning should be put to use!
You'll be the first to rate us. [Click to book.]
       Free tea & coffee. Space for bikes & skis.
       Quiet hours past ten. No children, please.

O For a Muse on Fire

and swatting at the flames with whatever
she can grab—a dish towel, September's
Ploughshares. O for a muse who sweats
real fear, smells her own singeing hair,
who seems suddenly capable of speaking
above a whisper. O for a muse on fire,
torching figure eights into my kitchen floor—
gold-sandaled dervish, perverse candle.
O to be the one who could save her,
   to take my sweet time with the water.

Baubo

Demeter's mourning was ending the world. *Cry on,*
called the rivers, flooding. Crops caught fire.
Her daughter gone, she was prepared to die on

her knife's point. Enter Baubo & her lyre—
bawdy friend to Demeter, first to twist her
cry into a laugh like rusting wire.

Mothers, women, when your hearts have blistered
remember there's a balm you can rely on:
a well-timed whisper from a wiser sister.

Smash Room

Our text thread pings, cajoling me to join
a hen night at the trendy local spot
where, for a fee, with safety gloves & specs
we're welcome to destroy a room of junk.
Staff stocks the space for us: discarded trunks,
old printers, vacuum cleaners long past work,
glass bottles, vases, mugs. A rocking chair.
I find a plate in my old china pattern
& hurl it with an unbecoming joy.
We crank house music loud, annoy the clerk,
& pose as we destroy cheap dinnerware,
then tag our cheeky photos #HardHatHot.
The whole thing's orgiastic—ersatz sex—
but it will do. Sometimes a girl must shatter.

The Drive-in Movie

Only some spy caper, something with flash
& tech & flesh, a film you & I can half-
watch as stars flick themselves on & off,
in need of a jump. Each car's radio is reading
the same script in a different voice, but we
unfocus our ears & hear the cinema chorus.
The crunch of gravel has called us here,
the queer night-cuisine of pickles & root beer
floats, the projected light so clean it makes
children of us. The air turns too chilly for me
but I forget to mind, while you don't even eat
the popcorn you are eating. The charged dark
blends the field of strangers & we all link arms
as we exit: you, me, & our intimate no one.

Strings

The banjo-maker's wife builds puppets
holding little banjos. She uses his scraps
of wood & extra varnish. I bought one,
a sad-eyed bear. I cannot hear its music.
What would it feel like to go home happy?

My days are badly joined & fall apart
when I am too rough with them. I should
make something new from their pieces,
maybe a toy that sings. I can make it dance
with strings, I will feed it from a real

baby bottle. Its eyes will open & close,
& it will sing the song of every night
I spend alone. The banjo-maker's wife
has a name. He speaks it when they finish
sweeping sawdust. It is almost a question.

The Artificial Ceiling

Midway through the renovation of the historic ballroom,
the foreman discovers 14 feet of forgotten height.

    In the 1970s, the ballroom's stewards installed a drop tile ceiling
    to save money, the grand room's volume being expensive to heat.

Decades later, architects squeal at this news. Their crews demolish
the artificial ceiling. Immediately the ballroom's posture straightens,

    eyes blinking open from under false eyelids as windows
    once believed to be half their true height are uncovered, towering

& dramatically arched with delicate iron traceries along the top.
Almost too much light now pours in—the designers sketch

    rich curtains but all parties refuse them, even while the startling new view
    from this second-story ballroom makes people feel they might tumble,

fall into the park below. Along the rib cage of the gently vaulted
ceiling are—have always been—3 stenciled circles in equal sizes. Once

    these stencils are restored, 3 sister chandeliers are ripped
    from other rooms, now drip from the hearts of the hand-drawn rings

& the ballroom is right. The air, the light, the overwhelming height.
From guests, always this remark: How could anyone hide this beauty?

    But I understand. If I close my eyes & stretch my arms overhead,
    I can rap my fingernails against my decisions, my past, the choices

that once protected me. I made them all with love, I hung each mistake
with care. Over time, I too forgot about the light no longer there.

My Grandmother Cannot Understand
Why I Would Want to Hear Her Birth Story

a found poem

Are you sure there's not some more interesting story
      you would like to write about?

Well like I said, I don't know many of the details.
      That's something that happens—when you get older, Erica,
      you wish you would have questioned your parents
      or your grandparents
      or your aunts & uncles—
            you wish that you would have talked to them more.
                But when you're young you're busy with your
                own stuff.

Here's all I know about the story that I was told.
      I was told this stuff from my mother,
            nobody else ever told me about it.
      Just my mom told me about it.

At the time, she lived with my aunt Hazel
      while my dad was in the Marines.
      He was in the Marines & he was, you know, not here,
      in Cincinnati or anything.
            And on a summer day,
                my mom decided to go up & visit with her
                mother,
                my grandma Kirschner, & she lived in
                Foster, Ohio,
                     which is not very far from
                         Cincinnati or from here.

It was just a typical summer day,
      & she was 7 months pregnant with me.

And in the afternoon she—
    she never told me much about going into labor,
    but I suppose that's what she did.
And there were no menfolk around,
    because they were either in the service, or they were at work.
    It was mostly just older men—you know,
        most of the men were in the service in 1944.

So she went into labor,
    and there was one neighbor man,
      an older man, an old man,
      she never told me his name or anything.
    But they did, you know, find him, & he took her to the—
      was going to take her to the hospital,
        and she told me that he drove an old "Willys car."
        I don't even know what that is.
        A Willys car.
        Willys.

He was driving her to the hospital,
    and I don't even know how close they got or anything,
    but I was ready to come out.
      So I came out, I was born—
        I looked on my birth certificate today—
        I was born at 3:15 in the afternoon.

Then they took her to Deaconess Hospital.
    I was already born. I was born early, Erica.
      I was not supposed to be born until August.
      And I was born June 6.

She was 7 months pregnant,
    and I weighed 5 pounds when I was born.
      I was in the hospital for 6 months after I was born.
      They did not have the up-to-date things

that they have now for preemies,
and I had milk in my lungs, she said.

And that's why I had to stay in the hospital
for 6 months. She said that her sister
had asked the doctor
about my chances of living,
and the doctor said
that he wouldn't give a nickel for my life.

But I did live.

The Getaway Car

for my niece on her first birthday

Look, little hell-raiser, I am not known for my natural way
with children. I've had to learn a lot since last October.
I thought your teeth came in too early, for example,
but it appears that you know best. You also know
my brother better than I ever did—when you're ready
I hope you will teach me your magic, how you transformed
my baby brother (who loved to chuck toy planes at our ceiling fan)
into your protective father. But today is *your* birthday, Fiona, & I am
meant to be giving you gifts! Your dad is no doubt expecting
Baby's First Book of Suffragettes or a cherry-red pocketknife
made for little hands. I want to believe I have something else
to pull from behind your ear, a tarnished copper piece
of wisdom I could never tell my brother. Just for us girls.
Today that task is beyond me, but here is what I can offer you:
When you collude with the moon & decide it is time to ask
a question, any question, my answer will be yes. Need help
conquering your very first unconquerable mistake? Yes,
I've untied my share of knots. Watch my hands. Are you ready
to make a little mischief, something to make your diary
worth hiding? I have ideas. (It is not safe to discuss them here.)
Eager to pierce whatever women are piercing in 2035?
Yes, I will know just the place—but dream bigger than that, Fi.
Get creative. Make me sweat a little. Lose a night's sleep
over the heft of your request. If you are anything like me,
you will find yourself in need of a getaway car. Ask me. Now,
go eat your celebratory peas. Please also find enclosed
a photo of your father when he was your age, a tin can
with 1,700 miles of string, &, why not, a pocketknife. Red.

Part of Me Hurtling Toward

found in	silence	part of me	that is	calling
foundering	answers	waited	me	out
part of me	pushing away	part of me	hurtling	toward
always	my intuition	waits	alone	(oh, I see her!)
still	asking, asking	still	hurting	only myself

If Ever There Were a Time for a Long Title This Would Be It

Throw out the old rules, even the ones you made for yourself. Especially the rules you made for yourself. Fire your guns in the air like a prospector. Run & jump but do not play. Or do play, because you have forgotten what is on fire, what is burning right up. You will often forget & the forgetting will startle you out of your little peace. This is a time for something new, for something you've been afraid to try— you have bigger things to fear now. Find a corner of your house you did not know was there. Maybe add a chair. Maybe see if the windows can open wider than you usually bother with. See if something in you can open wider too. Spread that rib cage wide & let a bird in. What the hell. There was a time when birds could not nest inside you, but who can remember that other life?

NOTES

"Daguerreo" is a golden shovel that borrows a line from Toi
Derricotte's "Speculations about 'I.'"

"Father as Ghost or Sheep or Nothing" is a golden shovel that borrows
a line from Anna Ahkmatova's "Imitation from the Armenian," as
translated by Stanley Kunitz & Max Hayward.

"Nivôse" is an homage to Jane Hirshfield's "The Stone of Heaven."

"Smash Room" is what A. E. Stallings refers to as a cat's cradle sonnet,
which scatters its rhymed couplets across the poem.

"My Grandmother Cannot Understand . . ." is a direct transcription
of a story my grandmother Hazel recalled for me over the phone.

"Part of Me Hurtling Toward" is a form that Kat Lehmann calls a
sudo-ku, forming haiku both horizontally and vertically.

ACKNOWLEDGMENTS

I'd like to thank the following journals in which these poems first appeared, often in slightly different forms.

Birmingham Poetry Review ("Deciduous")
Broadsided Press ("Pelt")
Cherry Tree ("Nocturne after Kelly Weber")
Colorado Review ("Each Night I Send My Courage Out" [as "After Rain"]; "Sestina Obbligato")
Foothill Poetry Journal ("Why Is My Angel So Small?")
The Inflectionist Review ("Preface")
The Lyric ("Wake-up Call")
The MacGuffin ("My Grandmother Cannot Understand . . .")
Ocean State Review ("Father as Ghost or Sheep or Nothing"; "Ghost Man on Second"; "Invitation")
Twenty Bellows ("The Drive-in Movie")
Willawaw Journal ("The Getaway Car"; "Links")

"If Ever There Were a Time for a Long Title This Would Be It" first appeared in the anthology *The Great Isolation: Colorado Creativity in the Time of the Pandemic.*

"Smash Room" was published as a cowinner of the 2023 Maria W. Faust Sonnet Contest.

"Disorder" was selected as the winner of the 2021 Yellowwood Poetry Prize by judge Matthew Olzmann and published in *Yalobusha Review.*

"Five-Story House" and "Shucking" were published by and named finalists by *Tinderbox Poetry Journal* for the 2023 Brett Elizabeth Jenkins Prize.

WITH GRATITUDE—

To Dan.

To West Chester University Poetry Center, which awards the Donald Justice Poetry Prize, part of the Spencer Poetry Awards, and to Mark Jarman, who selected my manuscript and—though he flatly denies it—changed my life. (Thank you to Amy Jarman for taking my side.) To West Chester University Poetry Center's Director, Cherise Pollard, and to West Chester University staff members Nancy Pearson and Cyndy Pilla, as well as to the past winners of this prize, many of whom have warmly welcomed me into this honored lineage. To the Spencer family. To the poet Donald Justice.

To Autumn House Press, and especially to my kind, attentive, and thoughtful editors Mike Good and Christine Stroud.

To the faculty and students of the Western Colorado University Graduate Program in Creative Writing. Special thanks to Tyson Hausdoerffer, Maya Jewell Zeller, CMarie Fuhrman, Clemonce Heard, Steve Coughlin. To my own cohort, as well as the students before and after our class who became friends and mentors. Unrelenting thanks to my thesis adviser, Julie Kane, whose fingerprints I can trace throughout this collection, particularly in her suggestion to turn to myth during my sonnet crown. Julie is also a previous winner of the Donald Justice Poetry Prize, and I will continue to follow in her footsteps any chance I get.

To the poets I consider teachers whether or not we shared a classroom, including but not limited to Diane Seuss, Dan Beachy-Quick, Jericho Brown, Leila Chatti, Camille Dungy, Matthew Olzmann, Steve Scafidi, and A. E. Stallings.

To Sara Bryan. Cindy Hohman. Amy Catanzaro. Kris & Jen Cole. Kate Kimble. Nancy Beauregard. Linda Vescio & Tony Joern. Brian Palmer.

Finally, to my family: Hazel; Kimberly; Ryan, Jenny, James, Kayleigh; Bradley, Kristine, Fiona, Rustin. Jan, Phil; Jenny, Eric, Sully.

ABOUT THE DONALD JUSTICE POETRY PRIZE

The West Chester University Poetry Center welcomes submissions of unpublished, original book-length manuscripts that pay attention to form for consideration in this competition.

Since 2018, Autumn House Press has published the Donald Justice Poetry Prize winning manuscript. The Donald Justice Poetry Prize is part of the Spencer Poetry Awards at West Chester University.

The following list indicates the winner as well as the judge:

2018: *The Last Visit* by Chad Abushanab, selected by Jericho Brown

2019: *Voice Message* by Katherine Barrett Swett, selected by Erica Dawson

2020: *No One Leaves the World Unhurt* by John Foy, selected by J. Allyn Rosser

2021: *Out of Order* by Alexis Sears, selected by Quincy R. Lehr

2022: *The Scorpion's Question Mark* by J. D. Debris, selected by Cornelius Eady

NEW AND FORTHCOMING
FROM AUTUMN HOUSE PRESS

Murmur by Cameron Barnett

Ghost Man on Second by Erica Reid
Winner of the 2023 Donald Justice Poetry Prize,
selected by Mark Jarman

Half-Lives by Lynn Schmeidler
Winner of the 2023 Rising Writer Prize in Fiction,
selected by Matt Bell

Nest of Matches by Amie Whittemore

Book of Kin by Darius Atefat-Peckham
Winner of the 2023 Autumn House Poetry Prize,
selected by January Gill O'Neil

Near Strangers by Marian Crotty
Winner of the 2023 Autumn House Fiction Prize,
selected by Pam Houston

Deep and Wild Places: One Life in West Virginia by Laura Jackson
Winner of the 2023 Autumn House Nonfiction Prize,
selected by Jenny Boully

Terminal Maladies by Okwudili Nebeolisa
Winner of the 2023 CAAPP Book Prize,
selected by Nicole Sealey

For our full catalog please visit: http://www.autumnhouse.org